1-Volleyball was invented in 1895 by William G. Morgan in Holyoke, Massachusetts, USA.

2-Volleyball is the national team sport of the Philippines and is often played on the streets and beaches of the country.

3-Originally, volleyball was called "Mintonette" before taking its current name.

4-Volleyball is a sport where strategy and coordination are as important as brute strength.

5-The first official volleyball match was played on February 9, 1896.

6-Volleyball is one of the few sports where teams can score points without having the serve.

7-Volleyball has been an Olympic sport since the 1964 Summer Olympics in Tokyo.

8-The volleyball is designed to be lightweight and aerodynamic, making it ideal for quick rallies.

9-Beach volleyball is also an Olympic discipline, introduced at the 1996 Summer Olympics in Atlanta.

10-Volleyball is played by millions of people as amateurs, whether on the beach, in parks or in the gym.

11-The volleyball is usually made of leather or synthetic materials and weighs around 9 to 10 ounces.

12-Volleyball players may touch the net, provided it does not affect the game.

13-Volleyball teams are made up of six players on the court at a time.

14-Beach volleyball has its own specific rules, including the ban on touching the net.

15-Volleyball teams can only score points when their team serves the ball.

16-The "lob" is a technique used to thwart the opposing defense by hitting the ball gently over the net.

17-Volleyball matches are generally played in three winning sets, with each set played first to 25 points.

18-The "center" is a player who is in the middle of the net line and is often involved in blocks and quick attacks.

19-Volleyball players must rotate clockwise when rotating to serve.

20-Volleyball is taught to young people to develop their agility, coordination and reflexes.

21-The most powerful attack in volleyball is called the "spike" or "smash."

22-The Beach Volleyball World Championships attract mixed teams from countries around the world.

23-The "libero" is a player specialized in defense and reception, wearing a jersey of a different color from the other players.

24-Volleyball has a rich history with legends of the sport, like Karch Kiraly, considered one of the greatest beach volleyball players of all time.

25-Rally scoring is used in many volleyball competitions, meaning that a point is scored in every rally, regardless of which team is serving.

26-The "red card" is a severe sanction imposed on players for unacceptable behavior on the field.

27-Volleyball is one of the most practiced team sports in the world.

28-Volleyball is a sport where the team that makes the fewest mistakes often has an advantage.

29-Brazil is one of the most successful nations in volleyball, with numerous Olympic gold medals.

30-The "disadvantage" is a situation where a team is in a defensive position after a powerful smash from the opponent.

31-The Russian national team is also very competitive and has won many medals in international volleyball competitions.

32-Volleyball was first included in the Special Olympics in 1975.

33-Japan is the birthplace of beach volleyball and has won numerous Olympic medals in this discipline.

34-The number of touches allowed for each team before returning the ball over the net is generally limited to three, with the exception of contact on the block.

35-The Youth Olympic Games also include a volleyball competition, which aims to promote the sport among young people.

36-Beach volleyball is often played on fine sand and must meet specific standards regarding sand depth.

37-Beach volleyball is generally played in teams of two players.

38-Volleyball referees use hand signals and whistles to indicate decisions and infractions.

39-Volleyball is a very popular sport in schools and universities around the world.

40-Volleyball is an inclusive sport that allows players of all sizes and skill levels to participate.

41-The "pancake" is a defense technique where a player places his hand flat under the ball to save it from hitting the ground.

42-Volleyball players must be versatile, because they are often called upon to play in different positions during the match.

43-The "digger" is a player specialized in receiving powerful opponent smashes.

44-Rotation in volleyball means that each player must move in a specific sequence after each point.

45-Volleyball is also a Paralympic sport, with teams of people with disabilities competing at the highest level.

46-The "side switch" is a common practice in beach volleyball, where teams change sides of the court after a certain number of points to balance the advantages of sun, wind, etc.

47-Volleyball is one of the most inclusive sports, with mixed teams and teams for people of all ages.

48-Volleyball is a demanding sport in terms of endurance, with matches that can last a long time and players who must remain alert.

49-The "kill block" is a technique where a player successfully blocks the ball and lands it in the opposing court.

50-Beach volleyball is often considered more physically demanding due to the sand, which provides additional resistance.

51-Volleyball is often associated with strict rules on ball contact, including double contact and carry.

52-Volleyball is a highly televised sport and widely broadcast during major international competitions.

53-Volleyball is a physically demanding sport, requiring considerable agility, strength and endurance.

54-The setter is often considered the brains of the team, because he makes quick decisions about distributing the ball.

55-The International Volleyball Federation (FIVB) is the world body that governs the sport.

56-The "clutch player" is a player who excels under pressure, scoring important points in critical situations.

57-Volleyball is played in more than 200 countries around the world.

58-The "dig" is a defensive skill which consists of receiving the ball hit by the opponent.

59-Beach volleyball, in addition to being a competitive sport, is also a popular recreational sport on beaches around the world.

60-The "libero" cannot block or attack the ball above the net, but he can defend at any height.

61-Volleyball is one of the fastest sports in the world, with rallies lasting just a few seconds.

62-Volleyball is one of the sports where players are likely to make spectacular dives to save the ball.

63-The vertical jump is a crucial skill in volleyball, as players must jump to block, attack and defend.

64-Volleyballs are often customized with specific colors and logos for competitions.

65-The "lineman" is a term used to refer to a volleyball player who plays behind the baseline and is usually an excellent server and receiver.

66-The setter dump is a technique where the passer pretends to distribute the ball and keeps it to score a point.

67-Volleyball has a passionate global fan base, with many supporters attending professional and international matches.

68-Volleyball is a sport where non-verbal communication is essential, with manual signs to indicate the actions to be performed.

69-Volleyball has naval roots, as it was originally designed as an indoor game to entertain sailors during the winter.

70-Beach volleyball is played on a smaller court than indoor volleyball, with a lower net.

71-The "sideout" is a term which designates a situation where the serving team wins a point.

72-The "jumbo" is a larger than average player who is often used to block opposing smashes.

73-Volleyball has a variation called "Sitting Volleyball" where the players sit on the ground.

74-The "pipe" is an attack where a player hits the ball from behind the court.

75-The first volleyballs were made of cowhide.

76-Volleyball is a sport of hand-eye coordination, requiring precise passing and well-timed attacks.

77-The rules of volleyball have evolved over time to include specific rotations of players on the court.

78-Beach volleyball players often wear sunglasses to protect themselves from UV rays reflected from the sand.

79-The first volleyball world championship took place in 1949 for men and in 1952 for women.

80-Volleyball is a sport that requires great agility, as players must move quickly around the court to react to balls.

81-Volleyball is a communication-intensive sport, with players using signals and shouts to coordinate their actions on the court.

82-Beach volleyball is often played barefoot for a better feel of the sand and better grip.

83-International volleyball matches are supervised by referees who ensure the application of the strict rules of the game.

84-The line judge is an official who monitors the court lines to determine whether the ball is "in" or "out."

85-Volleyball is played on a rectangular court measuring 9 meters by 18 meters, divided into two camps on each side of the net.

86-Beach volleyball players sometimes use wax to improve their grip on the ball.

87-The baseline of the volleyball court is also called the "service line."

88-Volleyball is often played in gyms on floors specially designed to reduce impact on the knees and ankles.

89-The "rally point system" is used in many volleyball competitions, meaning that a point is scored in each rally, whether the team serves or not.

90-Volleyball is a sport that promotes camaraderie and team spirit, with players working together to achieve a common goal.

91-"Feinting" is a technique where a player simulates an action to deceive the opponent.

92-Volleyball is one of the most practiced sports in the world, with national federations in more than 200 countries.

93-Volleyball matches can last from a few minutes to more than an hour, depending on the intensity of the exchanges.

94-The "defender" is a player specialized in reception and defense, often positioned at the back of the field.

95-The spike is the most powerful offensive shot, with players capable of hitting the ball at impressive speeds.

96-Volleyball is often played indoors with a parquet floor for better grip.

97-The "dump" is a technique used by the passer to surprise the opponent by placing the ball directly in the opposing court.

98-Women's and men's volleyball teams are made up of six players each, but there are variations, such as mixed volleyball, where mixed teams are allowed.

99-Beach volleyball is often played barefoot for better grip on the sand.

100-The "block" is a technique where a player tries to stop the opponent's smash by jumping and placing his hands above the net.

101-Beach volleyball is subject to the elements, including wind and sun, which adds an extra dimension to the competition.

102-Volleyballs are constructed with a rubber bladder surrounded by layers of synthetic leather.

103-The "basket" is a technique where a player catches the ball above the net without touching it to block a shot.

104-The "center" is often the tallest player on the team, used to block opposing smashes and attack from the middle of the net.

105-The volleyball must be properly inflated, with a pressure of 4.3 to 4.6 psi (pounds per square inch).

106-Beach volleyball is often called "beach volleyball" and is popular on beaches around the world.

107-Volleyball is a sport that requires great coordination between team members to succeed.

108-The "net fault" is an infraction that occurs when players touch or pass under the net.

109-Female volleyball players generally wear jerseys and shorts, while male volleyball players wear jerseys and shorts or tights.

110-Volleyball is often played as an amateur in local leagues, clubs and tournaments.

111-The "set" is a technical gesture used by the passer to place the ball high for the attacker.

112-The "tip" is a technique where a player gently pushes the ball over the net to surprise the opponent.

113-The "libero" cannot attack the ball over the net, except in certain specific circumstances.

114-Volleyball is a very technical sport, with passing, receiving, smashing, blocking and serving skills.

115-Volleyball is also played in the gym, on the beach, on grass and even on snow.

116-Olympic volleyball champions usually receive gold medals, but this can vary from country to country.

117-The FIVB organizes volleyball competitions around the world, including the FIVB World Cup and the FIVB Nations League.

118-The "dig" is a defensive reception where a player dives to save the ball from an opposing smash.

119-Volleyball continues to evolve with new rules and technologies like video challenge to ensure fair decisions.

120-Volleyball players often use resin or powder to improve their grip on the ball.

121-Volleyball is one of the most practiced team sports in the world, with more than 900 million players worldwide.

122-The "quick set" is a rapid attack where the ball is distributed quickly to the attacking player.

123-Volleyball is particularly popular in Eastern European countries, such as Russia, Poland and Serbia.

124-Volleyball is a very popular sport in Asian countries such as Japan, China and South Korea.

125-The "libero" is often the captain of the team and plays a key role in communication on the pitch.

126-Rolling dig is a defensive technique where a player rolls after making a catch to keep the ball in play.

127-Argentina is one of the few countries to have a world-renowned men's and women's national volleyball team.

128-The "back-row attack" is a rule of volleyball which allows players from behind to attack the ball above the net in certain situations.

129-Beach volleyball is generally played in two winning sets, each at 21 points, with a 15-point tie-break if necessary.

130-The "dump set" is a technique where the passer pretends to give the attackers a play, but instead returns the ball to the opposing team.

131-Brazil is often considered the country of "beach volleyball," with many famous teams and Olympic titles.

132-Volleyball is a sport where precision is essential, whether for serves, attacks or passes.

133-Volleyball is included in the Pan American Games and the Asian Games.

134-The "swing block" is a blocking technique where a player blocks an opposing smash by keeping his hands moving.

135-Volleyball has a seated variation played by physically disabled athletes, which is a Paralympic sport.

136-Volleyball is a dynamic sport, with players constantly moving around the court to defend and attack.

137-The "kill" is a term commonly used to describe a successful offensive smash that scores a point.

138-The "five-one" is a volleyball game system where one player is designated as the main passer and remains in play during rotations.

139-Volleyball is taught in many schools as a sporting activity in its own right.

140-Volleyball is often played in indoor gymnasiums, but it can also be played outdoors on sand or grass courts.

141-Technology was introduced to measure ball speed and player movements, aiding in performance analysis and improvement.

142-The "spoon serve" is a serving technique where the server gently hits the ball over the net to make it fall into the opposing court.

143-Volleyball is a sport that promotes the growth and development of social skills, as it requires constant communication between teammates.

144-Volleyball is a sport where endurance and concentration are essential, as matches can be long and mentally demanding.

145-Women have competed in volleyball at the Olympics since 1964, while men have been included since 1964.

146-The "floating serve" is a serve where the ball has unpredictable movement due to its minimal rotation.

147-Volleyball is also a popular sport in college circles in the United States, with many universities offering athletic scholarships to talented players.

148-Volleyball is a sport that requires great coordination between team members to succeed.

149-The first beach volleyball world championship took place in 1987.

150-Touch is an infraction that occurs when the ball touches a player or object outside the field.

Made in the USA
Columbia, SC
22 August 2024

40993153R00041